# The [illegible]dge



*by*
*Alfie Lewis*
*and*
*Peter Lewis*

*Photography by Peter Lewis*

# *Dedication*

To my mother and father for their help in times of need and to my late instructor, George Wellington, who put me on the right path.


Peterson House,
Berryhill Industrial Estate, Droitwich, Worcestershire WR9 9BL

Sole World Distributors
Peterson Book Company,
Peterson House,
Berryhill Industrial Estate, Droitwich, Worcestershire WR9 9BL

Printed in England by
Worcestershire Web Offset Ltd,
Northbank, Berryhill Industrial Estate, Droitwich, Worcs. WR9 9BL

# *Foreword*

Of all the people that proliferate the martial arts today, one name surfaces time and time again. That name is Alfie Lewis of Liverpool Freestyle. This man's meteoric rise to fame has been nothing short of phenomenal. His dynamic fighting style and authoritative method of application has led his contemporaries to label him a sports karate genius. Alfie Lewis, not satisfied with becoming Great Britain's greatest freestyle tournament fighter, took his talents abroad and onto the international world circuits to become the World Allstyles Kickboxing Champion.

In 1987 in Munich West Germany at the WAKO (World Allstyles Kickboxing Organisation) World Championships his finely tuned precision fighting style in all the rounds, up to and including the finals of his weight division, caused the fifteen thousand strong audience in the Munich Olympic Stadium to rise to their feet and give this man a standing ovation for his incredible competition prowess. The audience, made up from over forty nations chanted 'Alfie Lewis OK' for more than ten minutes. Surely recognition beyond the normal peripheries for Alfie Lewis' razor sharp skill. His talents have been recognised on both sides of the Atlantic, not just for being a sport karate phenomenon of the eighties but also for rewriting the book on tournament fighting.

Alfie Lewis is a winner in the true sense of the word, having taken the first place slot in hundreds of tournaments during his career. Many believe his star has not yet risen, and the years that lie ahead are to be paved with still more successes on the competition floor.

One often wonders what his recipe is for such consistent victories that have almost become his trademark during this last decade.

Surely it just couldn't be technical excellence alone, that has allowed him to become the world's number one tournament fighter.

The answer becomes apparent when you meet the man. Alfie Lewis positively exudes PMA (positive mental attitude). It is this special ingredient harnessed with his incredible and advanced fighting skills that have taken Alfie to the top of the tree. He believes that anything is possible, if you are prepared to work for it. And work for it he has.

"Nothing that's any good comes offered on a plate". The expression would seem to suit Alfie Lewis perfectly. Only by effort, hard work, and an unswerving belief in one's own capabilities, can anyone ever hope to be a winner.

Alfie Lewis began life in the martial arts with western boxing at six years old and then moved across to Judo and consequently Ju-Jitsu some years later. When he was about twelve, he began training in Karate but again moved on to greener pastures. His next soujourn into martial disciplines was Kung Fu, when he was fifteen. In Kung Fu, Alfie Lewis had found the slot in which he felt most comfortable. Alfie felt more at home with the none rigid and flexible approach of the Chinese martial arts than he had done with karate. His instructor, almost at once sensing that he had more than just another beginner on his hand took a special interest in the boy and guided him along the path that would best display his natural talent and ability.

This total freedom of expression within techniques allowed Alfie, even though still young, to experiment with what he had been shown, until that particular movement developed along the course of Alfie's own natural body mechanics. And quite often emerged barely recognisable from it's original form. But this suited Alfie, and pretty soon he was applying these techniques on the competition mat to notch up a continuing series of tournament successes. Even Alfie didn't realise at the time, that he was laying down the early groundwork for the concept of freestyle or in simple terms that 'art of no style'.

Going off on a tangent, as it were with experimentation of standard techniques, suited the somewhat extrovert nature that best describes Alfie Lewis. Individualism within training, allows the fighter to step outside the normal confines of styles or systems. Then, those techniques belong to the person using them, and they don't become carbon copies of the instructor or coach that first taught them.

It was inevitable that with the number of competition wins that Alfie Lewis was amassing, he would come to the attention of the martial arts press. When this happened, he was dubbed the somewhat less savoury title 'the animal' probably due to his fighting style.

The name of Alfie Lewis and his team the 'Liverpool Freestyle' has become something of a battlecry on the open tournament circuits of this country. And when they fight everyone watches!

Within the last five years Alfie and his team have notched up nearly one hundred first places. No mean feat in itself, but when you consider that the Liverpool freestyle is not an association team but that all members come from that one single club in Liverpool's tough docklands area!

When they march out onto the competition floor dressed in their bright red suits, other lesser mortals perhaps sigh, and feel the twinge of impending defeat.

In 1983 at the WAKO World Championships at Wembley, Alfie Lewis became the World Lightheavyweight Semi Contact Champion after beating USA's Rudy Smedley in the final. At the following World Championships in 1985 he just missed retaining his world crown by being beaten, the guy he took it from two years earlier America's Rudy Smedly. But again in Munich another two years later he snatched back the world crown, only this time for keeps. Not satisfied with becoming almost a legend on the freestyle open circuits, Alfie Lewis crossed over the barrier between freestyle and traditional and gained for himself a place on the hughely successful British Karate Team, under the leadership of Ticky Donovan. This transition was made with so little effort on Alfie's part, he could have been born to it. Needless to say Europe and the rest of the world sat up and took notice when this genial giant took to the floor and vanquished all that came against him. In the pursuit of excellence and higher endeavours on the sporting scene one only had to follow the career of karate's greatest diplomat, Alfie Lewis freestylist extraordinaire . . .

# *Contents*


| | |
|---|---|
| *Introduction* | *1* |
| *The Art of Freestyle* | *3* |
| *Beginning the Edge* | *7* |
| *Honing the Edge* | *19* |
| *Sharpening the Edge* | *33* |
| *The Cutting Edge* | *45* |
| *On the Edge* | *56* |
| *The Winning Edge* | *68* |

# *Introduction*

My original intentions in putting together this book, is to pass on the bulk of knowledge I have attained throughout my many years in active competition on the tournament circuit. After perusing the bookshop shelves I found that there was a wealth of information on the martial arts but all centred around traditional karate. And yet the pulse of modern tournament karate is pumping in the direction of the freestyle movement. This book is aimed at all those forward thinking people who have had the strength and character to pull away from their roots in the traditional background and go forward under the banner of freestyle sport karate.

Freestyle karate is an entirely modern concept with a realistic outlook that is much more orientated towards the competition arena from club level to the international forum. It allows the individual his or her own free interpretation of techniques that are not hampered or bogged down with wasted movement. The icing on the cake being; that freestyle karate can make the transition from the sporting endeavours of the tournament floor to the life threatening street muggings that plague our society today. The techniques used in competition, and illustrated in this book can be applied with slight modification as a very successful method of self defence, in a street confrontation.

Freestyle Sport karate exemplifies the true spirit of what the martial arts are all about. In that it unites under one umbrella, in the spirit of brotherhood, all practitioners of martial disciplines in the name of sport. But at the same time the emphasis is directed at the aspects of 'the martial way' rather than just a sporting connotation. All techniques carry authority, let us not lose sight of this. To imply that freestyle karate is total sport would be a grave mistake. It is a fighting art 'par excellence'.

When I have competed in tournaments, contemporaries have levelled comments at me such as, 'I gave the opponent looks that could kill'. Not so! they misinterpreted my real aim, which is fighting with serious intent. There is a difference. And it is this difference that separates the winners from the losers. Your state of mind and mental attitude when entering the tournament arena is as important as your fighting capabilities. The two are inseparable, unless you are aware of this fact I am afraid that the best you can hope for is second place on the rostrum every time.

Through the training programme laid out in the pages of this book I hope to guide both the beginner and the keen competition fighter through the pertinent points of tournament fighting. In the hope that somewhere along this path the readers own interpretation of the techniques will surface, and one's own style will begin to develop down the avenue that best befits their capabilities, weight, height, etc. Then you too can confidently say, 'my style is freestyle'!

Remember, when you go out there onto the mat, you are out there to win at all costs. People only ever remember winners, second place doesn't count for anything. So now go forward with great intent and be prepared to try something different. Taste these techniques, play with them, live with them. When you find a combination that suits push it, and yourself to the maximum. Treat each mistake as a lesson, in this way your confidence doesn't get undermined. Take your training further than you have ever done before. And always remember 'a winner never loses, and a loser never wins'.

Good Luck!

*Alfie Lewis, 1989.*

# *The Art of Freestyle Karate*

When asked to describe what Freestyle Karate actually was, Alfie Lewis once said, "It is the style of the future". That comment made some years ago was certainly a prophecy that came true. As more and more traditional martial arts students are turning their training programmes towards the freestyle format.

Freestyle karate is more of a free flowing system of fighting, as opposed to the traditional rigid forms of karate. The manner in which Alfie Lewis conducts a class is much more toned down that than of the more heavy disciplined militaristic Japanese styles of karate instruction. He tries to create an atmosphere more akin to a boxing gym than a traditional dojo (training place for traditional martial skills).

Although discipline is maintained, as indeed it must be, it is not quite so restrictive or rigid. By this type of friendly approach it is found that students are more relaxed, and therefore not shy at coming forwards, in other words more receptive. Consequently this is reflected in their techniques. They are not afraid to make mistakes, so that when a difficult manoeuvre is attempted, they are not put off when or if it should go wrong.

Freestyle karate students learn how to kick and punch as do ordinary karateka, but not in straight lines up and down the gym or dojo, as the more traditional styles dictate. Instead, they adopt their own stances and practice techniques on each other lightly. To get the feel of a movement or to get inside that movement to see what makes it work or fail.

Students learn how to punch and kick but in the punching the techniques lean more towards the western boxing approach. The rigid hands seen in traditional karate are not for the freestylist. Unlike the "one on" punching technique taught by the traditional schools (left punch, right punch, left punch) Freestyle teaches a method known as 'swarming' or 'swarm punching'. This is best described as picking up a handful of stones and throwing the lot at your opponent. This way one is going to get through. Alfie Lewis fights in tournaments like this, all the time. He makes the attack so strong that no matter how well the opponent blocks you, he can't stop all of them coming in. An opponent faced with a swarm attack can easily be overwhelmed, and if it goes in hard enough, you can take away the opponents guard with little trouble.

Another method of punching in freestyle is termed 'blitzing'. This mode of attack is seen much more frequently today than it used to be. This is probably due to the advent of the freestyle movement. Always wanting to be a little different from his contemporaries, Alfie Lewis' blitzing technique is much more advantageous to the user because of the fighting strategy behind it. He advocates that when you punch, rather than go "one", you go in tight and punch, with the elbow going into their body at the same time as you punch. Many fighters are reluctant to execute a reverse punch in case they get hit. But by going in tight with the previously mentioned technique, if they do get hit, they usually only get it on the elbow which is effectively ricocheted off without any damage to the fighter. Although technically this particular technique is not allowed in active competition by leaving out the actual elbow strike, the technique is good enough to use instead of a straightforward block. Rather than block, you check them (the opponent), because the elbow is held tight in, you can go over the top and backfist the opponent as a secondary strike.

The freestylist's fighting stance is a lot higher and more relaxed. It is left to each student to find his or her own stance, once they have been shown and corrected into how to cover the body for an impending attack. It is more a case of being shown the music, but they have to sing the song. It is most important that whatever stance they adopt they feel comfortable in it, and that they can work from it with no difficulty.

The basic method for finding a stance is decided by the simple guidelines of, left leg falling forwards. This way, the student adopts a natural stance, rather than being forced into a stance that is completely alien to them. So the first point that strikes a visitor when first entering a freestyle class is that everyone stands differently, there is no uniformity about it whatsoever.

Because freestyle is built around the individual rather than an actual dictated style, it allows a kind of 'natural expression' to come through. In a way, this makes the instructors teaching job a little easier for the fact that instead of waiting for instructors when trying out something new, the student already knows whether or not it will work depending upon how awkward they feel with the given technique.

Alfie Lewis, when fighting, prefers his own defence of the leading arm down, working on the premise that what you can't see, you can't block. On the footwork side of freestyle, an important point to mention is that the heel is always raised on the back leg. In an attack, the leading leg pulls back first in the same way that a sprinter starts a race. Because the back heel is raised with the front leg pulled back (but firmly on the ground for balance) the fighter stoops low (this is termed low profile) and surges forwards with the full bodyweight behind the given technique. When pulling back on the leading leg, you pull back on the ball of the foot, rather than on the whole of the foot. In effect it is then like a spring with projection thrust gained from both the feet. So, in theory, for a fraction of a second the fighter is resting on the balls of each foot. It is perhaps this familiar surge forwards in competition that identifies the freestylist from the traditionalist.

The concept of meeting an opponent nearly square on as seen in traditional forms of karate is not the hallmark of the freestylist. In fact quite the contrary is observed. The freestyle student is taught to stand side on to their opponents, rather than face him directly. This method presents two points. First of all, by being side on you present less of a target for your opponent to see or strike at. Secondly, you don't have to turn your hips into the technique with your leading leg. It's there already. To kick, you just bring your leg immediately into action. Being so quick cuts down your opponent's reaction time to initiate a counter move. The only flaw in this method, if indeed flaw is the right word, is that it's antagonist's point out that it is much easier to be swept when in this stance. But I would perhaps point out that this is more due to the inexperience of the user rather than the inefficiency of the stance, although nothing is infallable. Alfie Lewis' answer to this flaw, is to streak in with a spinning hook kick.

In the freestylist's usable arsenal of techniques the parallel is often drawn between the traditionalist's reverse punch or (gyagazuki) and their own (freestylist's) backfist. The traditional man uses the reverse punch as his bread and butter technique whilst the freestylist's equivalent is the leading hand backfist. To the uninitiated, the use of the backfist by the freestylist resembles the traditional uraken or backfist in karate. This is not strictly true. The freestylist's backfist is delivered in a different manner altogether. This strike is usually gauged to get inside the opponents guard, rather than around it! It is a technique much favoured on the American points karate circuits.

In the area of kicking techniques one of the most favoured kicks to the freestylist is the round kick. Taken from the traditionalist's mawashi geri or roundhouse kick. But once again it is used by the freestylist in a different manner. Put simply, the roundkick is used very similarly to the backfist. It is a type of sliding round kick. At first sight it resembles a lazy kind of kick. This is probably due to the fact that it has a wierd principle of timing attached to it's execution.

Nearly three quarters of all the freestylist's techniques are done with the legs. When a freestylist executes a kick, that kick is never fully extended. Neither is full power injected into it. The same applies to the punches of the system. Traditionalists would perhaps raise their eyebrows at the thoughts of kicking without going to full extension but this is what freestyle is all about. It is a kind of shortcut to competence and technical skill. Also dominant in the freestylist's repertoire is the way they prefer to snap kick and snap punch everything.

In fact everything in freestyle seems to be quick and snappy. It is a fighting system aimed at one purpose, to win, either on the tournament floor or out in the streets. All the techniques are trimmed down to be effective and natural. So much so, that it has been viewed as a kind of streamlined karate. It is only by breaking away from the traditional mould that a fighter realises there is so much more to use than they have been using previously. Freestyle is like a hat, it has to fit you reasonably well before its effective use becomes apparent . . .

*Peter Lewis, 1989*

## *Chapter 1*

# *Beginning The Edge*

As with any physical endeavour, whether it is a combat sport or otherwise, the tools that you require to do the job are all housed within your body. So therefore that body has to be in good physical condition in order to carry out the task at hand. The body is the empty weapon, so it has to be honed into shape and only exercise, a good diet and healthy living can achieve this. Any training regime has to incorporate various exercise routines. These routines have a two fold effect, they not only prepare the body i.e. stretching the muscles and tendons etc in order to execute good kicks with height and dexterity, but they also prepare you mentally as well. Thus eventually attaining a state of combat readiness.

For the main part, this book is profusely illustrated with simple step by step combination techniques which are easy to follow and vary in degrees of difficulty of execution. Each chapter should be read carefully and the instructions and suggestions assessed, assimilated, and then applied. Remembering that old adage 'Nothing worth having is ever easy', implies that hard work, effort, and constant practice is required if one is to perfect the techniques shown in this training manual.

Don't rush into the next combination before you have fully understood the last one. It's not just a question of copying the moves in the picture strip and then quickly on to the next one. First of all get to feel each movement, assess it's potential as regards your own weight, height, build, etc. Each manoeuvre should feel smooth and flow from one to another. Don't be afraid to experiment, if for instance you feel more at home and comfortable, switching around a technique so that it doesn't resemble what's in the photostrip but feels relaxed and flowing, then try it your way. If it still feels OK grab a partner and play around with it. Make the shoe fit before you go out walking.

For ease of use each photostrip is depicted in it's entirity, and the necessary instructions are featured underneath each manoeuvre or combination. With pertinent comments by Alfie Lewis on each of the three dozen or so combination techniques in the book. These very important comments should be adhered to at all times. But also remember the combinations work for Alfie Lewis, that doesn't necessarily mean that everyone will work for you. So it is important that the shoe fits for you as an individual before you rush off and test them out on the tournament floor. It will be an obvious advantage if you can gain the help of a good training partner. This will aid in playing with each combination. Again, what works for him, may not work for you, as an individual it is up to you to find your own level of achievement, and please respect your training partner at all times.

Further on in the book Alfie Lewis discusses his own training exercise regime. If some of these exercises prove to be too much then water them down to suit your own muscular and stamina profile. Build slowly rather than fast, nothing is to be gained by rushing except certain failure.

Try, test, taste, each and every combination in order to assess which ones are the winning edge techniques for you. If at the end of this short course only three or four best befit your mode of fighting skills then do not be disheartened. Because in those four combinations are numerous permutations for you to play around with. Don't forget freestyle is the art of no style, so don't become a carbon copy of your neighbour. You are an individual, so train like one. Learn diligently these winning combinations and maybe one day the winners' rostrum will seem like home to you . . .

## *Light Exercise for Warming Up*

When first beginning to exercise at the start of each training session heavy physical exertion is not required. A gentle tone up or warm up is all that is necessary. Visualise the body as a car with a cold engine trying to start up first thing in the morning. You wouldn't suddenly dash off onto the motorway and do a hundred miles an hour plus. The car gently ticks over then pulls away in first gear. Treat the body in the same manner. Begin with light running on the spot. Obviously the exercise potentials are enormous so it is best that the reader uses his or her own commonsense and institutes their own preferred light exercise programme. Most people have their own concept at what their own bodies can take. So do not take the exercise programme you institute beyond those limitations. Suffice to say just get the heart pumping and a gentle perspiration beginning to appear. Ten minutes should be all that is required in order to attain this state.

### Extended Regular Exercise Programme — Weeks 1 to 10

When a beginner commences any exercise programme, if they have not been too physical in their lifestyle prior to this, they should build up a solid exercise regime slowly and gradually. Increasing the length and reps of each exercise weekly. For instance if an exercise states ten push ups, then do only ten every day for a week. It doesn't matter if you feel you can do more than this, ten is suffice for that week. The following week do twenty, and then add ten each week until you find a compromising level. Another point worth mentioning is don't stick to one type of sit up for too long as the body becomes used to the task you put before it, keep changing the variation of the exercises.

**Weeks 1 to 4**

A few samples taken from a typical exercise programme in sit ups and other assorted exercises are as follows. Sit ups touching the knees. This involves laying flat on the floor, and gently lift the back from the waist off the floor a few inches and touch your knees with the palms of your hands.

The sit up crunch: Again laying flat on the floor the legs are outstretched in front of you crossed, at the feet and ankles. You raise your back off the floor slightly (as in the previous exercise) and at the same time bring the knees up into the chest. This exercise is performed in a pumping action. During this exercise the only part of the body to remain on the floor is the base of the spine and the seat.

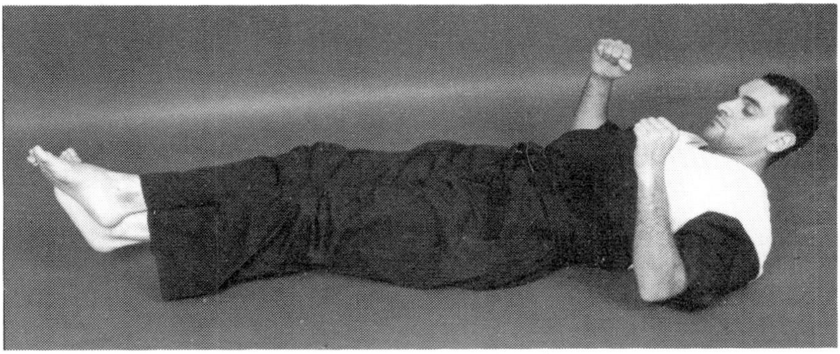

The Squat Thrust: This is the standard squat thrust exercise. You arrive at the press up position and in a hopping manner the feet jump towards the chest and then back out again.

Berpee's: Again similar to the previous exercise only after the hopping type jump that brings your feet to chest level, once the knees are tucked into the chest you then direct the body's energies upwards, by outstretching the arms and launching yourself into the air, with a jump. Upon landing, in the same spot, the feet squat thrust out again. And the exercise is repeated again.

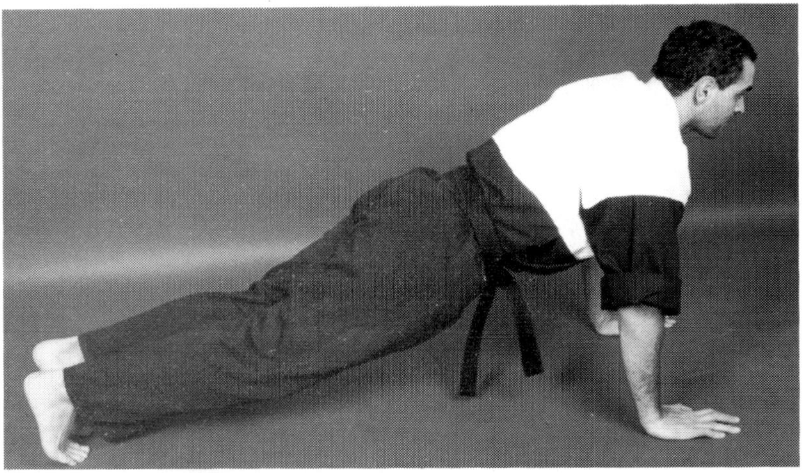

The programme is finished off with press ups.

After the first month, exercising on a regular basis, preferably everyday. The body will begin to be tonedup. Obviously the readers own exercises can be supplemented into the simple programme if desired. Within the first month introducing skipping into the plan will greatly aid in stamina build up and co-ordination. Beginners should aim for one minute skipping with a 30 second rest. Eventually working up to three minutes with no rest.

**Weeks 5 to 7**

As the body begins to get in shape, all the exercises in weeks 1-4 should be doubled up. Skipping should be increased to six minutes. The next exercise to be introduced is roadwork. But rather than jogging, concentrate on sprinting. Sprinting gives the martial artist 'explosive power'. The type of fighting that freestyle competitions demand, is in and out very fast explosive techniques.

The number of reps all depends on what you feel you can do comfortably. Say 50 yards to begin with, repeated five or six times, but only using about 80% of your power. These 50 yard dashes, are worked so that you run there and walk back, so that you get a chain reaction. Don't go crazy, just be aware of when you are running to get the legs stretching. After you have done the six at 80%, run the last four (50 yard dashes) at 100% your maximum effort. This sprinting exercise is always finished off with a light jog of about half a mile just to wind the body down.

At all times, be conciously aware of your breathing and try to regulate it as near to natural breathing as possible. In order to fit your training into the time you have available the indoor exercises can be done on alternate days to those of the sprinting. Alfie points out that one of the worst things you can do in training and one that is guaranteed to set boredom in, is to do the same thing day in and day out. It is better to try and exercise one day and leave the actual technique training until you get to the gym or club in the evening of the next day. A good work out programme should leave you very tired, so it would seem a little pointless to then go on for another two hours or so with your martial arts techniques, because you will be too tired to do them justice, and more than likely mess them up. If anything the heavy exercise should be done at the end of the class rather than at the beginning. And yet clubs all around the country still practice the heavy exercise session before the lesson begins. When all that is required is a light warm up and a fifteen minute stretch.

## *The Basic Stances*

Although stances in freestyle can be virtually anything that the user feels comfortable with and at the same time protects him from an attack. There are, what are best termed basic stances. These stances act as a platform from which to launch an attack or defend from one already initiated.

In competition and tournament fighting there are four common stances used **(1) The Basic Freestyle Stance.** This is a side-on positioned stance that offers the smallest target area to the opponent. And is probably the most used stance on the freestyle and open

circuits. The left arm is held low, to cover the rib cage, the right arm covers the chest, with the head turned up. Although the stance is popular it does lack a certain mobility.

**(2) The Natural Stance.** This is similar to a western boxers stance but a little more lengthened. The hands are held high as fists, again just like a boxer, at shoulder height. This stance is aimed more for mobility. But lacks the full protective cover-up as seen in the basic stance.

**(3) Reverse Hands Basic Stance.** This stance is the reverse of the basic freestyle stance, in that the hands are, left hand up, right hand down. As opposed to left hand down right hand up. Again in a side on stance. This stance presents a type of wall effect for the user, so that you get a total flank on one side of your body. The near side hand is raised above the ribs to offer the opponent a visible target area. This opening can sometimes entice the fighter in. As soon as he begins the execution of the kick, the defenders nearside hand, suddenly drops downwards from the air to protect the rib cage, the opponent has already initiated the move and committed himself. So the defender in the reverse hands stance lunges forwards and drives in with a reverse punch to his midsection.

**(4) Total Cover Stance.** The TCS or total cover up stance is reminiscent of how the great boxer Ken Norton used to stand. This

stance allows the fighter to bob and weave. It keeps the opponent preoccupied due to the fact that he can't see you changing angles, because your arms are constantly on the move it allows the user to open up his opponent and test his weak points. The stance could be described as a threatening gesture stance. He (the opponent) doesn't know what you are going to do next, so he has to keep on the alert. Whereas the user continually looks for an opening. It is a stance that can allow the user a certain amount of breathing space.

Although as mentioned, there are a lot more stances in the freestyle framework we have not shown any more because it is the books intention for the reader to perfect his own fighting technique rather than actually trying to teach a 'freestyle format' and producing carbon copies.

## *Kicks and Punches*

A recent survey on open competitions over the last few years has shown that the main scoring techniques are the reverse punch. The back fist, which in recent years has proved to be something of a winner and has come very much to the fore amongst competitors, and with the ridge-hand. The backfist is the fastest delivered hand technique possible. In the area of kicks, the leading leg mawashi or round kick has proven very successful. Which is quite the reverse of competitions of years ago when the back leg mawashi was de rigguere.

The side kick also known as the 'push kick' has come much more into it's own on the freestyle circuit, as opposed to the front kick from earlier traditional tournaments. These five techniques have been proven winners as the top scoring techniques on the world circuits.

Apart from these five techniques there are other kicks and punches used in freestyle but their success rate is not as high.

On the hands side, there is the uppercut. Not used by a lot of fighters because they haven't learned to control it too well or use it correctly. Then of course there is always the danger of hitting the opponent too hard with it and knocking him out, thus getting yourself disqualified.

The hooks, left hook, right hook, good scoring techniques which score on the WAKO competition circuit, but on the freestyle open circuit front they haven't caught on as much yet.

In the kicks the axe kick can be seen to be successful on occasion, but doesn't score that often. It is more commonly seen in taekwondo competitions than in freestyle tournaments. The spinning hook kick, and the jumping kicks family, shouldn't be neglected because they are part of the art, but although Alfie Lewis wouldn't tend to use these lesser techniques often, he does point out that they are good techniques to combine with something else to get a point. For instance execute an axe kick then follow through with a reverse punch for the point. So combined with something else they are effective.

Inexperienced fighters should not attempt to use the lesser techniques as one shot points scorers, or they could come unstuck. You have to learn to mix them, to set an opponent up. Again for instance, go in with a backfist then reverse punch, this gets the opponent leaning back and set up for an axe kick. Two of Alfie's favourite kicks is the jumping spinning back kick, and the jumping spinning hook kick. Which a few years ago on the open circuits, scored points for him on many occasions. But is no longer the secret weapon it once was. As many fighters have used it since and are now all educated in it's use, to the extent that fighters can now spot it coming in.

We now look at the various combination techniques within the freestyle system.

**Technique No. 1 . . . Front Hand Jab and Front Leg Round Kick**

Fighters square off both in left leg stance. Jab forwards to the face and then bring the front leg up and kick to the head.

**Points to watch . . .** *Stay as far behind the jab as possible, keep your body behind the jab. When you bring the back leg up don't lean forwards presenting your chest to the opponent. Stay side on. Don't let your back leg fall out of line with the front leg as this can turn your body to a disadvantage. Keep the back leg directly behind the front leg. Keep your jabbing hand slightly extended, this can help in pushing your opponent off, so that he can't come over the top and deliver a counter blow.*

**Technique No. 2 . . . Reverse Punch Backfist Same Hand**

Fighters square off, left side forwards. Attacker attacks with a reverse punch right hand to opponents stomach. Defender either moves back to avoid or tucks in to avoid. Thus the attacker loses some distance. To make up the lost distance the attacker twists his body more around tucking his right arm back to cock it for a backfist, then delivers backfist to opponents head.

**Points to watch . . .** *When delivering the reverse punch rather than rushing in, you inject yourself in, don't throw it in. Keep the body behind the punch all the time.*

# *Chapter 2*

# *Honing The Edge*

## *Advanced Exercise Programme for Tournament Build Up.*

A gradual programme that Alfie terms a competition build up is done over a period of six weeks. Weeks 1 and 2 is a medium programme build up, followed by weeks 3 and 4 which is a little more strenuous, culminating in weeks 5 and 6 with the advanced work out. Which should take the fighter to his peak fitness ready for the competition. Knowing when to peak is very important to your performance on the mat. Normally you would peak about half way through the final week. At this stage the fighter rests two days before the tournament.

Any competition fight demands a great deal of energy and stamina of the participant. In order to maximise on every ounce that your body has to offer, and to ensure that you don't run out of steam in the final few seconds of a very important final, you have to over train on the stamina side. For instance, if you were to fight a three round match then an ideal build up would be skipping for three minutes, for each of the rounds. So a nine minute stint of skipping helps prepare the body for this ordeal, having a 30 second rest in between each of the three minutes. An important point in all training, is that wherever possible lay a mat down, or some type of spongy rubber surface, this get's the body used to moving around on such a surface. Many fighters spend hours training on a hard wooden floor in gyms and clubs etc, only to go into a competition and execute those same techniques under stress against an opponent on mats. This sometimes has an alien feel to it, or at worst it can even slow you down. So remember mats are important when training.

Now advanced competition fighters reading this may comment that it's easy to do nine minutes of skipping. But as Alfie points out the problems with skipping for too long is that you begin to pace yourself. By pacing the analogy is drawn whereby if you are going on a marathon run which is 26+ miles long. You don't break out into a sprint at the start and maintain that pace throughout, otherwise you would be burnt out before getting halfway round. So the runners pace themselves in order to complete the distance and finish. But because freestyle competition is instantly demanding energy wise, you need the sudden burst of energy to be maintained for two minutes. Therefore your training has to reflect that use of sudden energy (burst energy) and to keep it up the distance of the fight. So again, if you are only fighting two or three rounds, or two minutes at a time, it's pointless training to last ten rounds or so. You have to maximise and condense the energy and stamina into that first two minutes and give it everything you have got. It is short term maximum energy explosion, that has to be concentrated on.

Next comes bagwork, again three rounds, three minutes each round, with 30 second rest intervals between each round. Exercise with basic punches and kicks, but don't use the bag in the standard martial arts mould or method of training, i.e. stepping back and kicking. Move around continually firing off shots, and looking for openings. Get used to the impact of your hands and feet connecting with a target. A heavy bag is not necessary, a light one will suffice, suspended from the ceiling if possible. This type of training will aid in the area's of, distancing, timing, penetration of shots. Again, three by three minute rounds.

Next comes step ups, these are done on a bench or small stool. With the previously mentioned mats under your feet step up on the bench and then back down, right leg, left leg, a hundred to begin with. This gets the lactic build up going in your legs. When you are fighting on mats in the competition area, the calfs of the legs take a lot of pressure not found in ordinary training in a gym on a wooden floor.

Following this comes the knee lift. Standing on one leg raise the knee as high as you can up past the waist to your chest, if you can, and then clap your hands in front of the raised knee. Quickly dropping down on to the other leg and repeating the exercise. In a one two rhythm this exercise should be done 100 times.

Then comes the situps, the first being "V" situps. Lie flat on the floor in the standard situps position, pull up from the waist and at the same time raise the legs to come forwards into the body (keep the legs straight) to finish up with your body resembling the letter "V". Do this ten times.

Swing situps. Again adopt standard sit up position, raise the legs into the air, keeping them locked at the knees and begin moving the legs back and to, as though walking down the street. Do 40 of these.

The final situp exercise, is the head raise. In the standard position just raise the head from the floor and execute a chin to chest movement. Do this 100 times, ensuring that the mouth is closed at all times.

**Knee Lifts**

**"V" Situps**

The next exercise involves lying on the stomach with a partner holding your legs, put your clasped hands behind your head, and begin to raise the body (from the waist) as far as you can. And then back down to the floor. Do this twenty times.

Next is the bar jumps. Construct a device at home or in the gym that resembles a limbo pole, a length of wood across two stools will do, raised about a foot from the floor. Jump over the pole, but sideways on not frontways on. Again, make sure mats are on either side of the pole.

The next exercise is the knees to chest in the air. This involves standing on the spot and jumping into the air clutching both knees into your chest with the hands. Upon landing, don't stop, begin again, keep up a bouncing rhythm. Do ten, rest for 30 secs, and then another 10.

Finally comes training with the focus pads. Get someone to hold the focus pads, preferably the ones with the white spot in the centre and just lightly move around hitting them. This improves and trains co-ordination and speed. When training with the pads hit them with everything in your repertoire, hooks, jabs, ridgehands, backfists, kicks, etc. The partner moves around continually, making the task just that much harder. But this difficulty improves your overall technique 100%.

In the advanced exercise programme of weeks 5 to 6 you will notice 'run' (front and back), the back run is initiated when you run forwards for a short distance then twist around and run backwards as fast as you can for a count of ten or twenty. This greatly under-emphasised exercise gets the body attuned to moving backwards at speed. This particular exercise pays off a hundredfold in competition.

Many fighters tend to train and exercise all in the same direction, this may prove well and good until the day of the tournament. Unfortunately all fights don't always move forwards on the matted area, so being used to backwards and forwards manoeuvrability equips you for anything an opponent throws at you. One point that should be mentioned, in training for this backwards running exercise, check beforehand nothing is behind you, otherwise, when going backwards you will have a tendency to look behind you to see if all's clear and if that habit is then taken into the competition area, your opponent will whack you as you turn around to see if you are going to stumble over anything. So when running backwards, always look forwards. In Alfie's advanced programme for this exercise three miles is advocated. So it would perhaps be best to use the perimeter of the training area at the club or a local park.

In the padwork for weeks 5 and 6 use fast combinations utilizing both hands and feet. Really work the bag, blast off techniques with intent and authority. Again, create openings and really get in there punching and kicking. Do this for three minutes at a time with thirty second rest intervals in between. When it comes to the padwork, treat them the same as the bags. Only this time it is your partner that dictates the pace. Concentrate upon accuracy, and speed.

Another exercise, a particular favourite of Alfie's is the 'cat lick'. This resembles an elongated type of press up. The movement is visualised something like an aircraft that is coming in to land then suddenly going back up into the air again. You glide into this movement. Do twenty of these. The last exercise of the session is the star jump. You jump from a squat position into the air as high as you can throwing both your arms and legs out as wide as possible. The finished movement resembles the body looking like a letter 'X'. Do twenty of these.

## *Pre-fight Training Advice*

The above advanced training session is terminated two days before the actual competition. Presuming that the tournament is on a Sunday, the last full training day is the Thursday. On the day prior to the tournament a good thirty minute stretch is all that's required, plus of course a good night's sleep.

### *Diet*

Because of the duration of many tournaments, which can be anything past eight long. Maintaining strength and energy levels is very important, but what does a competitor eat on the day of the competition, and for that matter is it safe to eat anything?

This particular area is obviously the subject of much controversy. So the guidelines have to be whatever you feel suits you and are comfortable with. But for reasons of proven worth. Alfie's own diet system may be of interest. The evening before the tournament 'packs up' this term refers to eating good solid food that is rich in both protein and carbohydrates. Which includes chicken and rice, wholemeal bread. A point to be mentioned here is the taking of vitamin supplements, throughout your training it is advised that you supplement your daily diet with vitamins. This area as we know can become something of a jungle to the uninitiated. So it is perhaps advisable to get a good book out on the subject to check out your own requirements. Alfie perhaps suggests an athletes vitamin super pack, which is a pack of multivitamins of high potency dosage and add to this vitamin C.

Upon rising on the day of the tournament a bowel movement is advised. Bearing in mind the standard of food in most sports centres, and maybe having to wait six hours or more before fighting. It is perhaps advisable to bring food from home. Chicken drumsticks, fresh orange juice (in carton), apples or oranges. Just something to nibble on whilst waiting for your turn. Sucking Dextrose tablets can also help the sugar balance levels in the body, especially as the fighter is under a certain amount of stress on the day of the tournament.

A light breakfast of a cereal or scrambled eggs is a good start to the day, rather than eat nothing at all, which could prove harmful by around five oclock in the evening.

In the area PMA (positive mental attitude) treat your mind to anything that builds up a positive approach to the days activities. For instance if you have a favourite suit, uniform gi, wear it, or a lucky talisman, in fact anything at all that helps build up the positive side of your nature. This will help to cast out doubt and the harmful negative vibes that one often feels under stress.

The power of this is perhaps proved by remembering the film 'Pumping Iron' with Arnold Swartzenegger. He hid Lou Ferregno's lucky tee shirt, and this upset the 'HULK' star so much, that Ferregno actually lost the competition. So a little eccentricity like that can have a powerful motivating force.

It is important to realise that while waiting for your turn on the mat, the body is continually burning nervous energy at a very rapid rate. This wasted fuel has to be replenished if one is to perform to peak efficiency. Don't try to survive the days fighting purely on orange juice and dextrose tablets. Even if it means eating something at the sports centre like a hamburger. What you eat that day isn't going to affect the rest of your life! And you'll probably burn it off anyway through nervous energy and normal body heat loss. Remember pressure, stress, and nerves, are all out to defeat you long before you ever get to face your opponent.

When Alfie Lewis makes it to the finals of his particular weight category (as he usually does) the time lapse between his semi final and the final can often be a few hours, he uses that time to have a shower, if local facilities allow. This helps him feel fresh, and makes him feel good. He keeps warm, so that when the fight begins he is not starting on a cold engine as it were.

## *Competition Build Up Six Week Period Chart*

| | |
|---|---|
| *WEEKS 1 and 2* | |
| STRETCH | 15 minutes |
| SKIPPING | 3 minutes (3 times) |
| BAG WORK (hands and feet) | 3 minutes (3 times) |
| STEP UPS | 100 |
| KNEE LIFT | 100 |
| CRUNCH (sit up) | 25 |
| "V" SIT UPS | 10 |
| SWING SIT UPS | 30 |
| HEAD RAISE | 50 |
| BACK RAISE | 20 |
| PAD WORK | 2 two minute rounds |
| *WEEKS 3 and 4* | |
| STRETCH | 20 minutes |
| RUN | 3 miles |
| SPRINTS | 5 consecutive 100 yard dashes |
| SKIPPING | 3 minutes (3 times) |
| STEP UPS | 100 |
| BAR JUMPS | 30 (done in 3 lots of ten) |
| CRUNCH SIT UPS | 50 |
| "V" SIT UPS | 20 |
| SWING SIT UPS | 50 |
| BODY TWIST | 3 (of 1 minute each duration) |
| KNEE TO CHEST | 20 |
| SQUAT THRUST | 20 (done in two lots of ten) |
| PRESS UPS (standard) | 20 |
| *WEEKS 5 and 6 ADVANCED* | |
| STRETCH | 30 minutes |
| RUN (front and backwards) | 3 miles |
| SPRINTS | 6 consecutive 100 yard dashes |
| SKIPPING | 4 lots of 3 minutes |
| BAG WORK | 3 three minute rounds |
| PADS | 3 three minute rounds |
| CAT LICKS | 10 |
| BERPEES | 10 |
| KNEE TO CHEST | 30 |
| BAR JUMPS | 40 (done in 4 lots of ten) |
| STEP UPS | 100 |
| BODY TWIST | 3 (of 1 minute each duration) |
| MIXED SIT UPS | 200 |
| BACK RAISE | 40 |
| STAR JUMPS | 10 |

***All training is best done on mats.***

**Technique no 3 . . . Front Leg Round Kick & Reverse Ridge Hand**

Fighters square off, left leg forward. Attacker slides in to attack with leading leg round kick to opponents head. Opponent blocks with his leading hand and attempts to counter with reverse punch with his right hand. Attacker blocks down against the reverse punch with his left hand and counters with a reverse ridge hand.

***Points To Watch . . .*** *When attacking with the leading leg round kick, don't let it fall down, as you come down. Always recoil and then place the leg down, otherwise you will fall onto any oncoming technique and get scored against. Block the opponents counter reverse punch as you are landing, don't land first and then block, because that split second can make all the difference. If you block the opponents counterpunch downwards, if he is rigid enough you will make him jerk forwards into your next technique.*

**Technique no 4 . . . Jab & Backfist (samehand) then Reverse Punch**
Fighters square off, left leg forward. The attacker, attacks by jabbing to opponents face, at the same time he shuffles forward with his leading leg. After the jab, the attacker rolls his left arm back towards himself, and still moving forwards backfists his opponent. Continually pushing forwards driving the opponent back, then reverse punches him.

***Point To Watch . ..*** *Don't get too close on your distance. On the initial jab and backfist you have got to sell them correctly. If they are not sold correctly, the opponent won't move back. He has to believe you are actually going in wth a determined jab or a backfist.*

**Technique no 5 . . . Reverse Punch Ridge Hand**

Fighters square off, left leg forwards. Attacker goes in with a reverse punch to opponents mid-section. Then he steps through with his right leg to his own left hand side. Then follows through with the same hand executing a ridge hand strike to the opponents head. At this stage the attacker should be on the opponents right flank.

***Points To Watch . . .*** *When attacking don't go into your opponent, but divert slightly to your left otherwise you will be too close too soon. In effect it's as though you were going to run past him. In running past him, thats when you deliver the ridge hand strike. Making sure that your left hand is covering, just in case he tries to fire off a shot at you. The cover hand acts as a safety device for counter attacks. The reverse punch strike converts into a ridge hand to finish the attack. This technique is a fine example of explosive power sprinting. As mentioned in the training in Chapter 1.*

**Always remember, every technique scores a point, if it hits! Even 'fakes' or 'feints', if the opponent falls for the first technique, even though you may be only setting him up for a second or third strike combination. So it is important to treat all techniques as if they mean business.**

**All techniques, even the basics, must be delivered with the positive confidence of commitment!**

**Technique no 6 . . . Backfist — Lean Sweep Takedown with Follow Through Punch**

Fighters square off left leg forwards. The attacker attacks with a long backfist, in order to push his man back, (as seen in the previous technique) as his man moves back, at one stage of the retreat the attacker brings both his legs together. The attacker then follows through with either left or right leg (depending on the position of the opponent) in a sweeping manner and takes both legs away from his opponent. Aim for both legs, if you catch them both it's good, if you catch only one of them he will still go down. The sweep is initiated on the opponent's calfs or anywhere midway between the ankle and the back of the knee. The attacker uses his shin to take out the opponent's legs.

***Points To Watch . . .*** *Watch the fake or the test backfist, that makes the opponent backpeddle. Fake him, if he doesn't move back, then its more than probable that he isn't going to fall for the technique, so forget it. When you are sweeping him and he is going down make sure that you're not that close to get tangled up in his clothes as he goes down, otherwise he could take you down with him.*

**Technique No 7 . . . Front Hand (Ridge Hand) Reverse Punch**

Fighters square off left leg forwards. Attacker attacks with a lunging front ridge hand. Because the technique goes in a circular motion, your opponent won't side step you, he will lean back. This makes his torso lean forwards, because his head leans back. As his torso pushes forward, attacker lunges forward with left leg and plants himself firmly on the floor, and power in with a strong reverse punch to opponent's now exposed mid-section.

***Points to Watch . . .*** *This technique has to be executed in a very rapid quickfire pace. Because you are doing a wide circular motion with the ridge hand, it does leave the attacker open and exposed for that split second. So you have to travel low and fast. Don't let your ridge hand lift you up, keep low with it. If the opponent does spot the attacker's momentarily exposed area, it is more than likely he will shot in with a reverse punch. this is perhaps best countered with a swat downwards block.*

## *Chapter 3*

# *Sharpening The Edge*

We open this chapter with some worthwhile exercise routines that may be perhaps termed 'Game Plays'. These game plays are aimed at sharpening the students/fighters technique and ring craft (generic term applied to fighting area).

These strategic exercises, which are taught on a regular basis down at Alfie's Liverpool club centre around a student encompassing every type of eventuality (combat wise) that they are likely to encounter on the mat in active competition. By being well versed in problem situations, his students when actually faced with a similar circumstance in a tournament, find little difficulty in coping, because they have done it so many times before during training.

These games not only make a wonderful diversion from the day to day routines and rigours of training, but can also be a lot of fun, whilst at the same time 'sharpening the edge'.

The built in psychological aspects of these Game Plays, allow the fighter to feel at home in the arena, and as near as possible, puts them under the severe pressure that they would be under whilst competing in an actual tournament. The advantages of these exercises is that they act as a mid-way fighting stage for beginners. In other words rather than just learning the basic techniques and then going into the arena and firing them off blindly, it gives the fighter more of a strategic way of thinking and behaving under pressure, and not wasting applied techniques.

Many students of the martial arts train regularly for competition in their clubs and gyms only to find that when they get into the arena their fighting balance/techniques/and ring skills differ greatly from what they have been working on for so long in the month's previous to the competition.

All the following games should be played in a regular sized area, just like that of competition and tournament. This is to get the students used to working within the lines all the time.

***1) Priming the Reverse Punch***

The rules of this game are that both sides can only use the reverse punch to score a point. Students square off in a simulated competition state. They can only strike with the reverse punch, they cannot block with the same hand. The block comes from the leading hand, but again, they can't strike with their leading hand. You can change stance as often as possible, but no kicks are allowed whatsoever, or for that matter any other technique save for the reverse punch. It becomes more and more difficult, since both sides know what technique is to be delivered. As the game progresses, both fighters know that they have to be both cunning and cautious to get their punch in. The whole thing takes on a game play whereby the fighters don't deliver erratic techniques, each move is carefully thought out, though both are under extreme pressure. It becomes a thinking mans game, like a game of chess.

***2) Kicking***

This game is similar to the first, but this time both fighters are only allowed to kick. The only hand techniques used are blocks with, no striking or punching allowed. All attacking must be done with kicks. Both fighters square off, then begin. A referee is used to score the points. Usually up to ten. This game gets the competitor used to someone coming in at them delivering a myriad of kicking techniques. Which is something you don't see too much of on the open circuits, where hand's are used to a great extent. When a fighter comes in using nothing but kicks, it gives the student/fighter a sharper eye for assimilating, assessing, and countering kicking techniques. You become used to the onslaught of legs being constantly thrown at you, within the face and body area. For the person kicking, it makes their job harder for the fact that they can't use their hands to set the kicks up, as is quite often the general norm. The attacker has to be able to kick and outwit you with his legs only. So this brings into play the attributes of body shifting and focusing.

***3) Defence and Counter***

The objective of the defence and counter game is to put one competitor constantly on the attack, and the other man on the counter-attack. Although this is self explanatory, it means that the defender cannot throw a defence technique until he has been attacked by the opponent. The idea is for the defender to be constantly on the move to try and lose his man (attacker) and wait for the attack before going in with a decent counter. The defender whilst on the move brings into play his faking/feinting abilities, in order to sucker the attacker to strike in the wrong place, and then counter sharply with all the right answers.

A point to remember is that the attacker must not get within a ridiculous range, i.e. too close. Otherwise this is not realistic of actual competition tactics. So keep a realistic distance between you and the opponent at all times. The counter attacker must always live on their nerves, because the attacker may come in with two fakes before an actual committed technique.

Another interesting objective within this game is for team fighters. You are practising (within a game) in case you are in a real competition situation as a member of a team. And your team is up on points, and you have to defend your lead (points wise). It doesn't necessarily mean that if you are on a team you do not have to go out there and win your own match. If the team is in front on points, this game gives the practice for you to defend your lead, a kind of play safe tactic.

***4) Slipping***

In the slipping game, you have two fighters, one man is an all out attacker, the opponent is an all out defender. The objective is for the defender to move, evade, and use any counter block he needs to avoid getting hit. He never actually strikes back in a defence. His sole aim is to manoeuvre around so as not to be hit. A third man is involved, by standing on the sidelines with a board, writing down how many times the defender gets hit with a good clean technique by the attacker. Each time the defender plays the game his objective has to be cut down the amount of strikes scored upon his person.

This game gets the student used to handling that pressure all the time, and learn to work out instantly, intricate counter moves such as slipping and faking. Even though the attacker knows that you can't counter, if the defender fakes his body, the attackers natural inborn instincts will be to move back, so this gives the defender space in which to move around and avoid a strike. So this is an important game to get the fighter used to working under pressure.

***5) Pulling Back***

This game involves two fighters facing each other, one is two points down, the other is three points up. So the beginning score is 5-2. In the set time allowed, the fighter that is behind must pull back those three points or even overtake his opponent. The man who is in front on points has to increase his lead, or failing that, hold the lead. This simulates to some extent the conditions of a team fight situation. Because the one fighter has to go out and hold that 5-2 lead, because the team needs it. Or the other way round, the fighter needs the three points to get a draw or a win for the team. So this particular game stresses the pressure put on both the fighters, rather than on just one of them. Either fighter can use any tool (technique) they want in order to gain the advantage. The pulling back game draws upon all the other afore mentioned games, to aid the fighter in completing his task.

*6) Working the Line*

The next game is working the line. One man holds the focus pads, it is his job to keep the second man moving around continually. The only problem is, that the second man has to keep one foot permanently on the line (one of the four lines that make the square (area) in which competitors fight). It is usually the backfoot that stays on the line. He is not allowed to take control of the centre area at all. Although his backfoot is allowed to move up and down the line, in any direction but must never come off it. The fighter with the focus pads will move around chasing the fighter. So the line man has not only got to stay on the line, but also must counter attack from the line and hit the pads accurately, throughout the two minutes duration of the game. Anytime the pads flick up, the line man has to hit the pads. This gets the fighter used to knowing where his line is and at the same time countering an attack. With training, the fighter on the line becomes very much aware of his boundaries, and it seems like a natural instinct takes over. Ultimately, knowing how to use your area, is like learning to live in the environment you have chosen for yourself, therefore the fighter copes better under stress and retaliation under pressure becomes almost second nature to him.

*7) Reflex Kicking*

Both sides have a focus pad in their left hands. The idea is that the first person will throw a kicking technique at the other. Either a roundkick, or back leg hook kick, the opponent must retaliate as quickly as possible with the same technique. So what you are actually doing is reading an opponent, and picking up on his technique. For instance, if you see someone do a backfist, you see the opening and get in there first with your own technique. It is perhaps best explained with the analogy that both fighters say, were on a piece of elastic. As the attacker jabs, as he draws his hand back the defenders hand follows it like a shadow. As though the attackers fist was actually drawing out the defenders fist, like a magnet pulling forwards.

*8) One on One*

One on one is like a copy cat game, where both sides face each other. The first person (who is designated to be first) can attack with any technique that he wants. Very similar to the reflex kicking game, but at a more advanced level. It is recommended that only fighters either with lots of tournament experience or who have thoroughly mastered the reflex game play this one.

As soon as the attacker has delivered his combination movements, the defender retaliates instantly with exactly the same manoeuvre. Both fighters work from combinations rather than single shot techniques. For instance if the attacker goes in with backfist, reverse punch, leading leg hook kick, come down and reverse punch again, the defender as soon as the the attacker lands, has to compute instantly what the attacker has delivered, within a fraction of a second and go back at him straight away with the same combination of techniques. This under practice, gets the fighters reflexes attuned to a very high level indeed.

The attackers strikes incidentally, don't actually land home, they just flick around you. The defender does not block, as the strikes don't hit him. Also the retaliation by the second fighter must be delivered in the same order as they came in at him.

In all these games the time durations should match the students experience and training capacity. Too much, for too long, too soon, only adds to confusion. It is better to approach each game as the fighters expertise allows, and limit the time durations to what is feasable for the fighters concerned.

**No 8 . . . Backfist Reverse Punch Round Kick**

Both fighters face off left leg forwards. Attacker strikes with a leading hand backfist to the defenders head. As the defender starts to retreat the attacker follows forward with a reverse punch to the midsection. As the defender further moves back, the attacker assesses the correct distance then follows through and executes a back leg round kick to the defenders head or body.

***Points To Watch . . .*** *As the attacker attempts to deliver the first of the combination (backfist) he pulls his leading leg back slightly so that his legs are closer together in more of a sprinting position. This will allow him the extra explosive spring forwards when delivering the backfist. Try and start with the heels raised, rather than raise them just as you go into the backfist technique. This saves a valuable fraction of a second. Otherwise if you start from a flat foot position, you have to raise your heels before executing the technique. Because of this type of 'sprint start stance' (as seen in chapter one) the fighter can move forwards at a much faster rate.*

*When finishing the attack with the round kick, don't leave your body square on. Get your body right around as quickly as possible, to prevent a counter attack from the defender.*

**No 9 . . . Side Kick Backfist**

Both fighters face off with left leg forwards. Attacker moves his back leg inwards, to commence the start of the sidekick. The defender leans back anticipating the kick. The attacker connects with the side kick to the defenders midsection. The attacker then recoils his kicking leg (left leg) and flips his body over the top, to backfist the defender on his head with a leading hand backfist technique.

***Points To Watch . . .*** *On the initial sidekick, make sure you are leaning far enough back, so that the defender can't charge you with a reverse punch. Also you are leaning back so that you can rock your hips forward for your later follow up backfist technique. As you sidekick your body leans out, as you backfist your body leans inwards. It is a type of seesaw action.*

**No 10 . . . Front Leg Sweep (Step Out) Reverse Punch, Roundkick to Body.**

Both fighters face off with left leg forwards. The attacker initiates a left leg sweep to his opponents leading leg. After he has swept the opponents left leg, he then steps across to his own left (out of range of retaliation) he fires a roundkick to the opponents body with his right leg, keeping his supporting leg bent to aid in his balance.

***Points To Watch . . .*** *Get far enough across so that you are not striking with your knee when you are stepping across to the side, otherwise if you are too close you are going to strike him (opponent) with your knee plus giving your opponent a chance to hit you back.*

*Also step far enough across so that you are not in the line of any counter attack. Make sure the sweep is enough to disturb the opponent, because if it's not enough he will just jam you and ram you as you move forward. Keep your guard moving around as much as possible as you are going forward so as to deflect any oncoming counters.*

**No 11 . . . Sidestep, Downward Block, Backfist Counter.**

Both fighters square off left legs forwards. The attacker attacks with a reverse punch to the defenders midsection. The defender sidesteps with the left leg to avoid the reverse punch. As a secondary precaution blocks outwardly, and downwards with his right arm again deflecting the reverse punch. The defender then checks the attackers punching hand with his own left hand. He then cocks his right hand in preparation for the backfist which is fired off to the attackers face.

***Points To Watch . . .*** *Make sure the side step by the defender against the attackers reverse punch is not too far over, and thus further expose your body area, and also allow the attacker enough distance to perhaps initiate a kick.*

**No 12 . . . Backleg Roundkick, Backfist**

Both fighters square off left leg forwards. The attacker begins the attack with a right leg, which is his backleg, roundkick to his opponents body. The opponent sees the oncoming kick and anticipating the power behind the kick is forced to block with his arm. As soon as he blocks, the attacker keeping his supporting leg bent, feels the block, drops in and fires off a rapid backfist to his opponents head, which will be on the opposite side. So the kick is to the right side and the backfist is to his left side.

***Points-To-Watch . . .*** *Try and keep both legs, the supporting leg and the kicking leg bent. It is not a full leg extension on the kick. If the attacking leg is bent, it does not allow the opponent a direct line of attack. If it's not straight, the opponent can block and come in. But by being bent, he (opponent) has to come around your kick to get at you. This is most important with this technique.*

## No 13 . . . Backfist, Reverse Punch

Both sides face off, the attacker leans back slightly with his foot pretty deep, to give the opponent the illusion that he is further away than he actually is. This is a typical trademark of the freestylist. The attacker then pulls back the leading leg, and leans in with the backfist high. Then follow through with a lunging reverse punch. But not a long reverse punch, keep it tight, and carry power and impact behind your shot.

***Points-To-Watch . . .*** *Try and keep the head low, don't carry the head high. All you want your opponent to see is your forehead. Keeping the head low cuts down his (the opponent) vision of your face.*

*Chapter 4*

# *The Cutting Edge*

The next two chapters feature combination techniques that are aimed at a more advanced level of technical ability. But as pointed out in earlier chapters the freestylist uses no limit as his limit, to take a phrase from the late Bruce Lee. If the beginner or intermediate students will be putting together their own various combinations of workable techniques, that suits them in particular. All freestyle student will be putting together their own various combinations of workable techniques, that suits them inparticular. All freestyle techniques can be used and mix matched to the user's own recipe of fighting style and format. If it works for you, use it!

**No 14.................................Forearm block, check, and backfist**

Both fighters square off in left fighting stance. Leaning slightly back, defender waits for attack. As the attacker strikes, the defender slightly pivot's his left heel thus throwing your left forearm into the oncoming reverse punch. Remember to keep your right arm high, behind your left forearm, to be used as a secondary blocking measure.

As soon as the defender feels the attackers reverse punch connect with the forearm, slap downwards with your right arm onto the oncoming reverse punch. Cock your left arm for the backfist and then fire the backfist off in a forward motion.

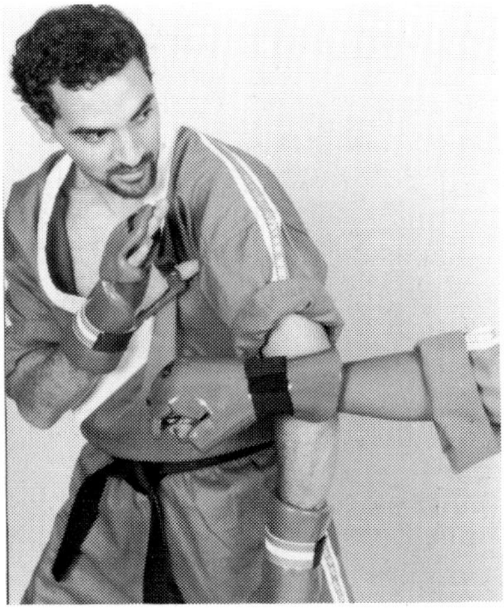

***Points to Watch.*** *When the defender blocks with the forearm and you twist your hips away from your opponent, don't turn your head away at the same time. This common mistake could cost you the point. Keep the head looking forward and your eyes looking forwards at the opponent all the time. Also try and keep your chin low, and behind your shoulder, but looking over your shoulder. Don't drop your shoulder to block, keep it high. In case the opponent follows through with a backleg roundhouse.*

**No 15 . . . Front leg fake, side hook kick, with roundkick finish.**

Face off to your opponent with a slightly more forward stance, more of a natural stance. With both hips pointing towards your opponent. Shuffle in, and fake a double hip twist to your left, trying to draw your opponent's attention to his own right hand side, to get him thinking you're about to attack on his right side with a hook kick or sidekick. Without stopping to give your opponent a chance to re-assess the situation or game play follow through the leg, recoil and then follow straight through with a roundkick to his head. What you are actually doing is faking a sidekick or hook-kick and then when it's too late for the opponent to realise it is only a fake, you convert the fake kick into a roundhouse and execute it. It is not two separate techniques, it's more like one long continuous one that's intermingled. The idea of the fake hook kick is to get the opponent going into your round kick. So when you fake the hook kick the opponent will move across the opposite way, which is a natural re-action on his part and as soon as he does this, you capitalise by following through with the round kick.

***Points to Remember.*** *Don't break the technique down into two movements, there is always a tendency to do this, don't! Keep the whole technique as fluid as possible. Also, try to keep your own defence on the roundkick, on the inside. Do not put your right arm behind the kicking leg, which is normal procedure for most martial arts, keep it on the inside, because that's where your attackers target is on you, because he is on the inside of your defences.*

**Remember Freestyle is the Style of no Style. Do not just copy these techniques, but play-around with them and find the combination which suits you best.**

**No 16 . . . Front leg front kick and backfist.**

Both fighters face off, this time right fighting stance. Prod out with your right arm as a feeler to judge or gauge the distance. Flick the front kick low so to make your opponent respond by leaning slightly forward. As soon as you feel touch contact on your foot with the block, withdraw the leg and begin to lean the top half of your body forwards so as to fire off a backfist. These are very tight techniques that should be executed at explosive speed. Not a one two action. The backfist goes in at the opponents face. Don't get high with the backfist, travel in low.

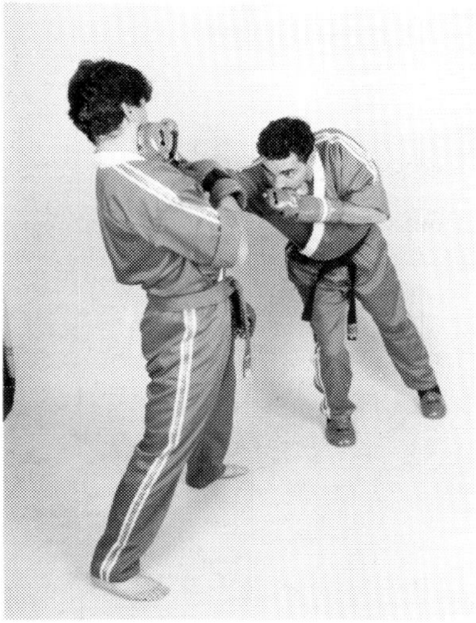

***Points to Watch.*** *Carry authority behind the backfist, because you are going forward.*

**No 17......................................Front leg round kick and backfist.**

Both fighters face off in a higher than normal stance. Attacker immediately fires off leading leg kick to the opponents left hand side. Drawing his defences over to his left. Thus leaving his right hand side open. Again, immediately follow through with a leading hand backfist to finish off the technique.

***Points to Remember.*** *Once you have kicked take time to assess if the opponent is going to come in with a counter. If the opponent does come in with the counter, then obviously the technique has got to be changed. If not, then follow through immediately with a backfist.*

**No 18....................Front leg sidekick (mid section) with roundkick.**

Both fighters square off right side forwards. The attacker immediately chambers his right leg so as to fire off a sidekick at his opponent's open midsection. Upon application of the sidekick, drag the supporting leg slightly so as to make any shortcomings in distance up. As soon as you feel body contact recoil the right leg, chamber it, making sure the knee is directly in line with the head and then fire a high roundkick to your opponents head.

***Points to Remember.*** *Drag the supporting leg in, so that your bodyweight is travelling with the kic. It shouldn't be just a static kick, the leg should be travelling slightly with the other leg that's kicking. also make sure that your kicking knee for your second kick is in line with your opponents head. So that you have a direct line of attack for your roundkick.*

**No 19......................Front leg roundkick with spinning hook kick.**

Fighters square off left leg forward, the attacker immediately brings his leg up, positioning himself for a leading leg roundkick to the opponents body. Slam the leg in, as hard and as fast as possible. As soon as the attacker feels contact, he withdraws the leg towards his right, and then starts to pivot. As soon as he (the attacker) starts to pivot, he gets his head around as quickly as possible. The attackers right arm also follows around as quickly as possible, but making sure the left arm is kept up to cover the face. The eyes should never leave the opponent for less than a quarter of a second. As soon as visual contact is made by the attacker, he then continues through with the spinning hook kick to the opponents head.

***Points to Remember.*** *Make sure the body kick does carry authority, so as to rattle the opponent (un-nerve him). Otherwise the opponent will have a thought about following through with a counter. Try to spin as quickly as possible, because it is a dangerous technique as you are showing your back for a split second. On the spin, as seen in photo No 4, the leading arm is out so as to carry anything that's there around, and in photo No 5 the arm takes out anything that's coming in at you. It is rather like a windmill action, then finish with the spinning hook kick.*

**No 20.................................Reverse punch, front leg hook kick.**

Both fighters square off in a reasonably high stance. The attacker moves in dropping his body weight a few inches. The attacker then fires a reverse punch off. As soon as body contact is felt from the reverse punch, readjust the stance by twisting the body onto the side, lining the opponent up with your leading leg and follow through with a front leg hook kick. Striking with the sole of the foot, in order to keep reasonable control and not damage the opponent. Make the kick a snapping kick using the knee for the snapping action. Don't follow through with the hips too much.

***Points to Remember.*** *On the reverse punch don't follow through with too much hip motion. Otherwise the attacker commits himself too much into the one technique (reverse punch). It is part of a flowing combination, so make it a snappy reverse punch, then immediately spin and follow through with the leading leg hook kick.*

*Between the hook kick and the reverse punch always keep in mind that the opponent has got a chance of hitting you. So keep your guard tight at all times. Keep the chin behind the shoulder, and the right arm down.*

## *Chapter 5*

# *On The Edge*

In this final chapter of picture strip techniques, we see that as in the previous chapter, these are also at an advanced level. When practising each combination manoeuvre, be sure to take note and read Alfie Lewis's own comments in the 'Points to watch out for' at the end of each combination picture strip. These are aimed at informing the reader about special points in delivery and execution of the said technique.

If a particular combination fails for you, before blaming the technique look very deeply into your own application and ensure that you are adhering to the manoeuvre step by step.

**No 21 . . . Angled Roundkick.**
Both fighters square off. Attacker is right side forward, defender is left side forward. The opponent is face on, his guard protecting both sides rather than his mid section. Attacker makes the move, left leg

round in a semi circle motion away from himself but towards the opponent on an acute angle. Attacker drags his right leg in the same direction as he is moving. Note the final position of attackers leg, before he fires the kick off. The attackers leg is then cocked and fired off in a roundkick at an angle aimed at the defenders head.

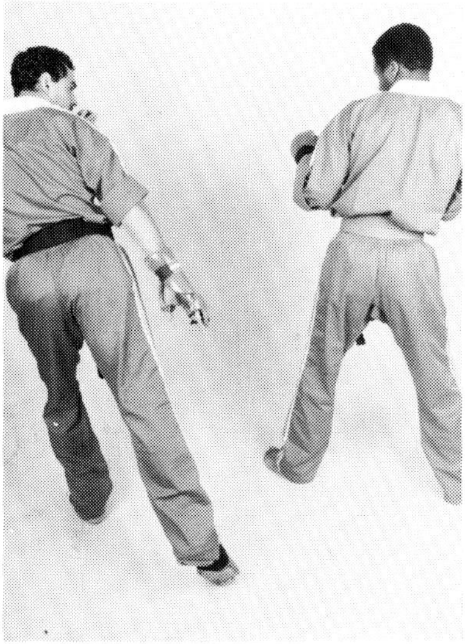

***Points to remember . . .*** *On the actual positioning of the legs when moving around at the start of the technique, remember to make it a skipping motion, it shouldn't be a stepping motion. Both the legs should move in this manner. The kick should not be forced, but rather continued with the momentum of the actual movement.*

**No 22 . . . Weave and Block, Sweep and Reverse Punch.**
Both fighters face off left leg forward. The attacker immediately attacks with a leading hand jab. Defender blocks with his back hand at the same time moving his head away from the oncoming punch. In one motion the defender simultaneously steps out with his right leg leaving his left leg behind. Then follow through with the left leg and drag the left leg up to take the opponents leading leg off him, to spread his legs. Don't sweep, but spread him. It's more of a dragging

motion than an actual sweep. The spread is executed either ankle to ankle or boot to boot. As soon as the opponent goes down, hit the exposed area wherever you see it with a reverse punch.

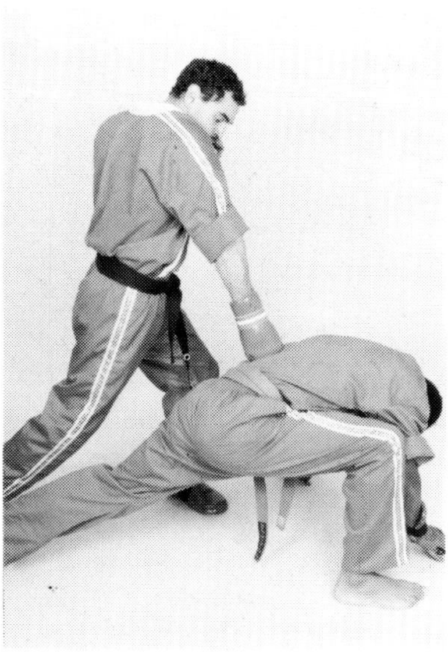

***Points to remember . . .*** *Again, re-emphasise don't sweep but drag. When you do step out, don't leave the left leg too far behind, try and synchronise it, so you are stepping and dragging all in one manoeuvre. Take the opponents leading leg, because when he jabs he distributes his weight onto his leading leg, so he is already pulled forwards slightly to start off with, thus making your job a little easier.*

**No 23 . . . Front Leg Hook Kick, Sweep, and Reverse Punch.**
Fighters square off. Attacker faces off, with his legs slightly more to his left. He immediately lifts the leg to the outside of his opponents righthand, in order to get the opponent to either lean back or move away. Then continue with the hook kick right the way round, making sure that after the kick lands, it places itself directly behind the opponents leading leg. As soon as the leg lands, the attacker ensures that his guard is tight and his eyes are forwards looking to the opponent. As the attackers leg lands, (behind the opponents lead leg) he lets his foot bounce slightly and takes the opponents leading leg off him with his (attackers) right leg, in a pulling forwards motion. The attacker immediately steps in, with his sweeping leg, and follows through with a deep thrusting reverse punch to the opponents mid-section.

***Points to remember . . .*** *Once the attacker has hook kicked, he must then maintain that tight (close) distance, he has attained with the kick. On the sweep, don't sweep outwards, sweep upwards. This is to up-end the opponents balance and bring him towards the attacker. This exposes his midsection area and makes him set up for the follow through reverse punch.*

**No 24 . . . Reverse Punch, Backleg Hook Kick.**
Fighters face off, left leg forwards. The attacker immediately pushes in a fast reverse punch to the opponents midsection, but keeping his own guard tight at all times. The attacker then pulls through his back leg, and places it in a cocking position for the hook kick. He (attacker) then fires off immediately the hook kick to the side of the opponents head.

***Points to remember . . .** When the attacker cocks his leg for the hook kick, don't pull the leg too far back, as to take it out of range of the opponent. Keep it to the centre of the opponent, so he can't charge the attacker in a counter move. If the foot goes too far around, the attackers area is left wide open. If the opponent does charge, the cocked leg acts as a blocking device to counter.*

**No 25 . . . Backfist, Spinning Backfist, Reverse Punch.**
Both fighters face off. The attacker fires off a leading hand backfist to the opponents left hand side. This is to get the opponent to block. As soon as the backfist is unleashed, the attacker doesn't wait around. He immediately starts the spin with his right arm. On the spin he tucks tight and fires off the spinning backfist. (These two techniques are to get the opponents guard going wide and set him up for the reverse punch). After the spinning backfist has been fired, the attacker continues the spinning motion right around, and follows through with a deep penetrating reverse punch.

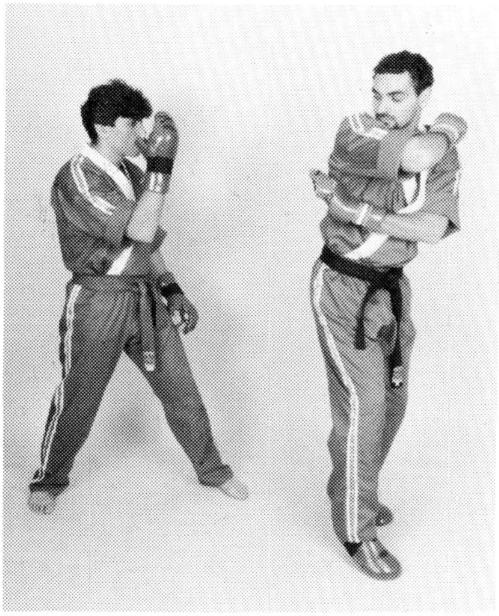

***Points to remember . . .*** *On the spinning backfist don't let the legs go too wide, keep them tight, otherwise you will find it hard to spin around. Keep every technique sharp and snappy, don't linger with them. The reverse punch is more of a whirlwind technique, that goes in deep. The success of this combination lies in the fact that it is not a commonplace or much used technique.*

**No 26 . . . Body Jab, and Spinning Hook Kick.**
Both fighters square off, in an upright position. The attacker suddenly drops his bodyweight low, and fires a jab in at the opponent's midsection, ensuring that his (attackers) head is low. The attacker leans into the punch so as to carry the bodyweight behind the jab. The attacker then immediately moves into the spin, cocks his right leg as high as possible, so as to keep the opponent off, and then unleashes the hook kick to the side of the opponents head.

***Points to remember . . .*** *This technique's success relies on the fact that the attacker is executing techniques both high and low, and that each shot carries full commitment. The first shot must carry authority, this keeps the opponent off you whilst you deliver the second technique which is executed at a snappy pace.*

**Remember . . . Mix and Match the techniques so you are an individual. Then no-one will know what you will do next.**

**No 27 . . . Reverse Punch, Backleg Round Kick, Reverse Punch.**
Both fighters face off. The attacker lunges forwards with a righthand reverse punch (at this point, emphasis must be placed on the word 'lunge') into his opponent's midsection. Also, the attacker stretches out his left arm in order to check the opponents guard, should he (the opponent) attempt to counter. This is a synchronised punching technique. The attacker immediately snaps his body back (into a safety zone) and then fires off a backleg round kick into the opponents head. The attacker then recoils his leg, and lowers it down behind the opponents forward leg. At the same time the attacker, leaning back (don't lean in) suddenly fires in with a reverse punch.

***Points to remember . . .*** *The first two techniques must flow as tightly as possible, the third technique can have a quarter of a second lapse, before it is fired off.*

*Chapter 6*

# *The Winning Edge*

We have seen in the previous five chapters the methods Alfie Lewis uses in both his training and active tournament fighting. The techniques illustrated have worked for him time and time again. In his final chapter we shall take a nostalgic look at Alfie's successes over the last few years. With comments from some of the worlds leading martial artists as to Alfie Lewis's superb fighting abilities. It is these abilities harnessed with hard work and tremendous effort that have set Alfie Lewis on his rise to eventually become number one in the world.

Alfie himself, often points out that there is no magical formula for becoming the best there is. Save for the fact that dedication to training and having an unshakeable belief in your own talents. Positive Mental attitude (PMA) in every endeavour not only puts the fighter into the major winners league, but also spills over into your daily life. That vibrant unmoveable faith in your own potential will then work in attaining life's goals outside the competition arena. To take a beginner and make him or her into a champion requires three aspects, which are, committment, PMA, and hard work. That is the secret of success and it is that secret that has given Alfie Lewis not only glory for himself but also to that of his club team the Liverpool Freestyle. The blade that cuts decisively both ways, is the blade that has the 'Winning Edge' . . . . .

## *Alfie's Major Titles*

| Title | Place | Year | Event | Result |
|---|---|---|---|---|
| British Open Kung Fu Champ | B'ham | 1977 | Pee Wee | First |
| WAKO European Championships | London | 1980 | Junior | First |
| British Semi-contact | B'ham | 1980 | Senior H/W | Second |
| KBI British Open Karate | Leigh | 1981 | Senior "A" | First |

| | | | | |
|---|---|---|---|---|
| Kodoki Open British Karate | Crewe | 1981 | Senior | First |
| SKU British Open Karate | Sankey | 1981 | Senior L/HW | Second |
| WAKO European Championships | Dublin | 1981 | Senior L/HW | Second |
| WAKO World Championships | Milan | 1981 | Senior L/H | Fourth |

| | | | | |
|---|---|---|---|---|
| British Semi Contact | B'ham | 1981 | Senior H/W | First |
| Kodoki British Open Karate | Crewe | 1982 | Senior Open | First |
| BKA British Open Karate | Bury | 1983 | Senior H/W | First |
| Combat Open British | B'ham | 1983 | Senior H/W | First |
| WAKO World Championships | London | 1983 | Senior L/H | First |

| | | | | |
|---|---|---|---|---|
| Prostel Tournament of Championships | Glasgow | 1983 | Senior L/H | Second |
| British Kung-Fu Championships | B'ham | 1983 | Senior | First |
| Champion of Champions | Coventry | 1983 | Senior H/W | First |
| Welsh Open Karate Championships | Cardiff | 1984 | Senior Open | First |
| Shindo Ryu UK Karate Championships | Leamington Spa | 1984 | Senior H/W | First |

| | | | | |
|---|---|---|---|---|
| Shindo Ryu UK Open Karate Championships | Leamington Spa | 1984 | Grand Champion | First |
| Champion of Champions | Manchester | 1984 | Senior H/W | First |
| SKU National Open | Altrincham | 1985 | Senior H/W | First |
| Combat Open (British) | Coventry | 1985 | Senior H/W | First |

| | | | | |
|---|---|---|---|---|
| Combat Open (British) | Coventry | 1985 | Champ H/W | First |
| UK Open Championships | Urmston | 1985 | Senior H/W | First |
| WAKO European Championships | Greece | 1986 | Senior L/HW | First |
| EKC English Open | London | 1987 | Senior H/W | First |
| WAKO World Championships | Germany | 1987 | L/HW | First |
| WAKO European Championships | Venice | 1988 | L/HW | Second (Retired injured) |
| WAKO European Cup | Venice | 1989 | H/W | First |

**"Alfie Lewis is the most versatile fighter I have ever seen in action. He can adapt to any type of fighting in any system. His versatility also extends to competing to any form of rules whether karate WUKO, semi-contact WAKO or kickboxing rules. It is my opinion that he is more than capable of becoming a great champion in any of these very specialized fields of combat."**

Bob Sykes

**"Alfie Lewis has long impressed me as being one of the finest martial arts competitors of his generation. Not only has he the physical ability and sheer ferocity to intimidate virtually any opponent, but he also has a keen understanding of the psychology of combat and an extraordinarily highly developed technical standard. Add to this the versatility that has made him a success in both points competition and the more regimented WUKO events, and you have a truly remarkable athlete. Perhaps the least acknowledged aspect of 'The Animal's persona is that he is, at heart, basically a nice guy, but I suspect that's the way Alfie likes it."**

Bey Logan

**"Having been born into the most humble environment in one of Europe's worst ghettos, he has risen above all that and, while having the ability to train and develop many championship tournament fighters, he has gone everywhere and put it on the line with all kinds of other people. He has recovered from very horrendous injuries and has still retained his ability to achieve top level results consistently. This surely must be the epitome of what a true martial arts character is supposed to develop."**

Gary Spiers

**"Alfie Lewis is Mr Ever Ready, he is a fight anyone, anywhere, at any time, type of person, and gives a 101% commitment on each occasion. As a permanent member and team captain of the Great Britain WAKO squad he is a source of continued inspiration for the team. His own positive mental abilities inspire fighters, that come into contact with him, onto greater things."**

Joe Johal, President WAKO Great Britain

**"Alfie Lewis apart from his very obvious talent and skill has never been one to lay idle in terms of competition. He consistently put himself and his many titles on the line, time and time again. A quality I most admire in him, unlike other so called champions."**
Sensei Roy Stanhope, 6th Dan

**"We've fought so many times I've lost count, we have set the tournament circuit ablaze time after time, Hell I'm qualified to say. There are champions and there are great champions. Alfie Lewis is one of the great champions."**
Kevin Brewerton

**"I think Alfie Lewis is one of the most talented people I have ever seen. Having trained him on the England squad I found him of good character. And on the WUKO side of karate I am only sorry we didn't have him with us for longer."**
David 'Ticky' Donovan, 7th Dan — England Team Manager and Coach

**"Alfie Lewis, in my opinion, is the finest semi-contact fighter in the world.**
George Bruckner's address to the audience at the WAKO World Championships in Munich 1987.

*Co Authors Alfie Lewis and Peter Lewis*